Lucy's Blue Day

Your Journal

Chris & Lisa Duke

"LUCY PEAR HAS WONDERFUL HAIR IT CHANGES COLOUR LIKE NO OTHER."

ALL ABOUT ME

Hiya!

So, you might not know my story...if you have, feel free to skip this section and move onto the next; if you haven't heard it, here it is in a nutshell:

My name is Lucy Pear. I have hair that changes colour depending on my emotions – a bit like a mood ring.

When I'm feeling my usual self, my hair is yellow (blonde).
When I feel angry, my hair is red.
When I feel jealous, it goes green.
And when I feel sad, it's blue.

It went dark blue once, and I didn't know what that was until I started speaking about it to someone who understood — my friend, Max. He helped me understand that all the feelings I feel are okay. It was really nice to have someone understand it actually.

One of the things I started doing was keeping a journal of my hair colour, what made me feel that way and why. It really helped me just pin down some of the reasons I was feeling the way I was and helped me understand them (and myself) a bit better.

That's why I've done this.

We're all in this together and writing your thoughts and feelings down will help you isolate moments where you've maybe not behaved like you normally would.

It's ok to feel anger, but it's not ok to lash out and hurt someone *because* I feel angry. I need to recognise that I'm feeling angry, deal with it, and figure out a way to calm down. I like to go to my room and listen to my music.

When I feel a bit sad, I like to watch a comedy with my besties or even play a game with my mum and dad when Brad (little bro) is in bed. I also like to talk to Max about things, because he gets it.

Hopefully this will help you the way it's helped me!

All my love,

Lucy xoxo

4

DON'T LET WHAT YOU CAN'T DO STOP YOU FROM DOING
WHAT YOU CAN DO — JOHN WOODEN

DATE: 03.04.2050

HAIR COLOUR: yellos

WHAT HAPPENED: I made POPPOB

WE ALL CAN DANCE WHEN WE FIND MUSIC, WE LOVE -
GILES ANDREAE

DATE: 04.045050

HAIR COLOUR: Bleu

WHAT HAPPENED: my mum didn't tell me she was geting up.

THE MORE YOU GIVE AWAY THE HAPPIER YOU BECOME –
ANTHONY MARITZ

DATE:

HAIR COLOUR:

WHAT HAPPENED:

I THINK I CAN. I KNOW I CAN — WATTY PIPER

DATE:
HAIR COLOUR:
WHAT HAPPENED:

IT'S NOT WHAT HAPPENS TO YOU, BUT HOW YOU REACT TO
IT THAT MATTERS - EPICTETUS

DATE:

HAIR COLOUR:

WHAT HAPPENED:

BEING KIND IS NEVER WASTED - SYLVIAN REYNARD

DATE:
HAIR COLOUR:
WHAT HAPPENED:

DATE:

HAIR COLOUR:

WHAT HAPPENED:

DO WHAT YOU CAN, WITH WHAT YOU HAVE, WHERE YOU ARE.
- THEODORE ROOSEVELT

DATE:

HAIR COLOUR:

WHAT HAPPENED:

DATE:

HAIR COLOUR:

WHAT HAPPENED:

DATE:

HAIR COLOUR:

WHAT HAPPENED:

DATE:
HAIR COLOUR:
WHAT HAPPENED:

IF WE AIM HIGH AND FALL SHORT, WE STILL ACHIEVE MORE THAN BY AIMING LOW AND FALLING SHORT. — UNKNOWN

DATE:

HAIR COLOUR:

WHAT HAPPENED:

REACH HIGH, FOR STARS LIE HIDDEN IN YOUR SOUL. DREAM
DEEP, FOR EVERY DREAM PRECEDES THE GOAL - PAMELA
VAULL STARR

DATE:

HAIR COLOUR:

WHAT HAPPENED:

NO ONE IS PERFECT — THAT'S WHY PENCILS HAVE ERASERS -
TERI CLAASSEN

DATE:

HAIR COLOUR:

WHAT HAPPENED:

SET YOUR GOALS HIGH AND DO SOMETHING EVERYDAY TO
MOVE FORWARD - UNKNOWN

DATE:

HAIR COLOUR:

WHAT HAPPENED:

WHEN WAS THE LAST TIME WORRY EVER SOLVED A
PROBLEM? BREATHE AND KNOW THAT YOU ARE PERFECT IN
THIS MOMENT - UNKNOWN

DATE:

HAIR COLOUR:

WHAT HAPPENED:

DATE:

HAIR COLOUR:

WHAT HAPPENED:

TODAY, BE THE PERSON OF YOUR DREAMS. SEE AND ACT FROM THEIR EYES - UNKNOWN

DATE:

HAIR COLOUR:

WHAT HAPPENED:

DATE:

HAIR COLOUR:

WHAT HAPPENED:

THERE IS NOTHING MORE IMPORTANT IN THE WORLD THAN
LOVING YOURSELF - BARBRA STREISAND

DATE:

HAIR COLOUR:

WHAT HAPPENED:

WHY FIT IN WHEN YOU WERE BORN TO STAND OUT? — DR.
SUESS

DATE:

HAIR COLOUR:

WHAT HAPPENED:

MOST TIMES, REGRETS ARE THINGS WE DIDN'T DO, NOT
THOSE WE DID - GAIL LYNNE GOODWIN

DATE:

HAIR COLOUR:

WHAT HAPPENED:

NEVER LET THE ODDS KEEP YOU FROM DOING WHAT YOU KNOW IN YOUR HEART YOU WERE MEANT TO DO - H. JACKSON BROWN, JR.

DATE:

HAIR COLOUR:

WHAT HAPPENED:

YOU CAN STEER YOURSELF ANY DIRECTION YOU CHOOSE — DR
SUESS

DATE:

HAIR COLOUR:

WHAT HAPPENED:

THE MORE THAT YOU READ, THE MORE THINGS YOU WILL
KNOW. THE MORE THAT YOU LEARN, THE MORE PLACES YOU'LL
GO – DR SUESS

DATE:

HAIR COLOUR:

WHAT HAPPENED:

NEVER GIVE UP ON WHAT YOU REALLY WANT TO DO. THE
PERSON WITH BIG DREAMS IS MORE POWERFUL THAN ONE
WITH ALL THE FACTS — ALBERT EINSTEIN

DATE:

HAIR COLOUR:

WHAT HAPPENED:

WINNING DOESN'T ALWAYS MEAN BEING FIRST. WINNING
MEANS YOU'RE DOING BETTER THAN YOU'VE DONE BEFORE –
BONNIE BLAIR

DATE:
HAIR COLOUR:
WHAT HAPPENED:

DON'T JUST READ THE EASY STUFF. YOU MAY BE ENTERTAINED
BY IT, BUT YOU WILL NEVER GROW FROM IT — JIM ROHN

DATE:

HAIR COLOUR:

WHAT HAPPENED:

DATE:

HAIR COLOUR:

WHAT HAPPENED:

CHANGE YOUR THOUGHTS AND YOU'LL CHANGE YOUR WORLD -
NORMAN VINCENT PEALE

DATE:

HAIR COLOUR:

WHAT HAPPENED:

WHEN YOU DO THE COMMON THINGS IN LIFE IN AN
UNCOMMON WAY, YOU WILL COMMAND THE ATTENTION OF
THE WORLD - GEORGE WASHINGTON CARVER

DATE:

HAIR COLOUR:

WHAT HAPPENED:

YOU MUST BE THE CHANGE YOU WISH TO SEE IN THE WORLD
- MAHATMA GANDHI.

DATE:

HAIR COLOUR:

WHAT HAPPENED:

DATE:

HAIR COLOUR:

WHAT HAPPENED:

THE SECRET OF SUCCESS IS TO DO THE COMMON THINGS
UNCOMMONLY WELL - HENRY J. HEINZ

DATE:

HAIR COLOUR:

WHAT HAPPENED:

SUCCESS IS NOT HOW HIGH YOU HAVE CLIMBED, BUT HOW YOU MAKE A POSITIVE DIFFERENCE TO THE WORLD - ROY T. BENNETT

DATE:

HAIR COLOUR:

WHAT HAPPENED:

ONLY THOSE WHO DARE TO FAIL GREATLY CAN EVER
ACHIEVE GREATLY - ROBERT F. KENNEDY

DATE:

HAIR COLOUR:

WHAT HAPPENED:

SUCCESS IS A STATE OF MIND. IF YOU WANT SUCCESS, START
THINKING OF YOURSELF AS A SUCCESS — JOYCE BROTHERS

DATE:

HAIR COLOUR:

WHAT HAPPENED:

IF I CANNOT DO GREAT THINGS, I CAN DO SMALL THINGS IN
A GREAT WAY – DR MARTIN LUTHER KING

DATE:

HAIR COLOUR:

WHAT HAPPENED:

ALL STUDENTS CAN LEARN AND SUCCEED, BUT NOT ON THE
SAME DAY IN THE SAME WAY - WILLIAM G. SPADY

DATE:

HAIR COLOUR:

WHAT HAPPENED:

THERE IS NO SUBSTITUTE FOR HARD WORK — THOMAS EDISON

DATE:

HAIR COLOUR:

WHAT HAPPENED:

IF YOU HAVE GOOD THOUGHTS THEY WILL SHINE OUT OF
YOUR FACE LIKE SUNBEAMS AND YOU WILL ALWAYS LOOK
LOVELY — ROALD DAHL

DATE:

HAIR COLOUR:

WHAT HAPPENED:

WE KNOW WHAT WE ARE BUT KNOW NOT WHAT WE MAY
BE — WILLIAM SHAKESPEARE

DATE:

HAIR COLOUR:

WHAT HAPPENED:

YESTERDAY IS HISTORY. TOMORROW IS A MYSTERY. TODAY IS A GIFT. THAT'S WHY WE CALL IT 'THE PRESENT' - ALICE MORSE EARLE

DATE:

HAIR COLOUR:

WHAT HAPPENED:

THERE ARE NO SECRETS TO SUCCESS. IT IS THE RESULT OF PREPARATION, HARD WORK, AND LEARNING FROM FAILURE — COLIN POWELL

DATE:

HAIR COLOUR:

WHAT HAPPENED:

WHEN WE FOCUS ON WHAT WE CAN DO INSTEAD OF WHAT
WE CAN'T, A WORLD OF POSSIBILITY OPENS UNTO US –
UNKNOWN

DATE:

HAIR COLOUR:

WHAT HAPPENED:

CHILDREN ARE NOT THINGS TO BE MOLDED BUT ARE PEOPLE
TO BE UNFOLDED — JESS LAIR

DATE:

HAIR COLOUR:

WHAT HAPPENED:

PLAY AND DON'T TAKE YOURSELF OR THE WORLD SO
SERIOUSLY. CREATE REASONS TO LAUGH! - UNKNOWN

DATE:

HAIR COLOUR:

WHAT HAPPENED:

IF YOU CAN'T FEED A HUNDRED PEOPLE, THEN JUST FEED ONE
- MOTHER TERESA

DATE:

HAIR COLOUR:

WHAT HAPPENED:

NEVER UNDERESTIMATE THE POWER OF AN UNLIMITED
BEING—YOU - GAIL LYNNE GOODWIN

DATE:

HAIR COLOUR:

WHAT HAPPENED:

NO ACT OF KINDNESS, NO MATTER HOW SMALL, IS EVER WASTED - AESOP

DATE:

HAIR COLOUR:

WHAT HAPPENED:

GO CONFIDENTLY IN THE DIRECTION OF YOUR DREAMS. LIVE
THE LIFE YOU HAVE IMAGINED - HENRY DAVID THOREAU

DATE:

HAIR COLOUR:

WHAT HAPPENED:

DATE:

HAIR COLOUR:

WHAT HAPPENED:

DATE:

HAIR COLOUR:

WHAT HAPPENED:

BEING DIFFERENT ISN'T A BAD THING. IT MEANS YOU'RE
BRAVE ENOUGH TO BE YOURSELF — LUNA LOVEGOOD

DATE:

HAIR COLOUR:

WHAT HAPPENED:

IF YOU CAN DREAM IT, YOU CAN DO IT — WALT DISNEY

DATE:

HAIR COLOUR:

WHAT HAPPENED:

GO MAKE YOUR LIFE THE ONE YOU HAVE ALWAYS WANTED,
KNOWING YOU HAVE THE POWER TO MAKE IT HAPPEN -
UNKNOWN

DATE:

HAIR COLOUR:

WHAT HAPPENED:

THE SECRET OF GETTING AHEAD IS GETTING STARTED – MARK TWAIN

DATE:

HAIR COLOUR:

WHAT HAPPENED:

WITH THE RIGHT ATTITUDE ANYTHING IS POSSIBLE — ROGER
CLEMENS

DATE:

HAIR COLOUR:

WHAT HAPPENED:

ACTION IS THE STEP MANY FORGET WHEN THEY WONDER
WHAT HAPPENED TO THEIR DREAM - UNKNOWN

DATE:

HAIR COLOUR:

WHAT HAPPENED:

YOUR EXPECTATIONS FOR ANY GIVEN SITUATION WILL
GREATLY INFLUENCE THE END RESULT - UNKNOWN

DATE:

HAIR COLOUR:

WHAT HAPPENED:

IN THIS VERY MOMENT YOU HOLD THE POWER TO CHANGE
SOMEONE ELSE'S LIFE FOR THE BETTER. GO DO IT - UNKNOWN

DATE:

HAIR COLOUR:

WHAT HAPPENED:

ABOVE ALL ELSE, BE TRUE TO YOU — WILLIAM SHAKESPARE

DATE:

HAIR COLOUR:

WHAT HAPPENED:

DATE:

HAIR COLOUR:

WHAT HAPPENED:

FIND PEOPLE WHO BELIEVE IN YOU UNTIL YOU CAN BELIEVE
IN YOURSELF – UNKNOWN

DATE:

HAIR COLOUR:

WHAT HAPPENED:

THE CLEARER YOU ARE IN THE VISION OF WHAT YOU WANT
IN LIFE, THE BRIGHTER THE SPOTLIGHT WILL BE TO LEAD
YOU ON THE RIGHT PATH - UNKNOWN

DATE:

HAIR COLOUR:

WHAT HAPPENED:

WE OFTEN LEARN TOO LATE THAT WE SPENT TOO MUCH
TIME WORRYING ABOUT THE THINGS THAT MATTERED LEAST
- UNKNOWN

DATE:

HAIR COLOUR:

WHAT HAPPENED:

IF YOU CAN'T CHANGE THE CIRCUMSTANCES, CHANGE YOUR ATTITUDE. FUNNY THING IS, WHEN YOU DO, YOU'LL FIND THAT THE CIRCUMSTANCES OFTEN CHANGE - UNKNOWN

DATE:

HAIR COLOUR:

WHAT HAPPENED:

DATE:

HAIR COLOUR:

WHAT HAPPENED:

KNOW THAT DEEP INSIDE, YOU ARE RESILIENT, BRAVE AND SO MUCH STRONGER AND MORE POWERFUL THAN YOUR FEARS - UNKNOWN

DATE:

HAIR COLOUR:

WHAT HAPPENED:

WE CAN GET SO MUCH FURTHER IN LIFE THROUGH
COLLABORATION RATHER THAN COMPETITION. ONE PLUS ONE
EQUALS ELEVEN, NOT TWO - UNKNOWN

DATE:

HAIR COLOUR:

WHAT HAPPENED:

THE SHORTEST PATH TO SUCCESS--FOCUS ON THE 'WHAT' AND
THE 'WHY', NOT THE 'HOW'. WORKS EVERY TIME - UNKNOWN

DATE:

HAIR COLOUR:

WHAT HAPPENED:

EVERY ACTION IN OUR LIVES TOUCHES ON SOME CHORD THAT
WILL VIBRATE IN ETERNITY - EDWIN HUBBEL CHAPIN

DATE:

HAIR COLOUR:

WHAT HAPPENED:

IF YOU HAVE GOOD THOUGHTS THEY WILL SHINE OUT OF
YOUR FACE LIKE SUNBEAMS AND YOU WILL ALWAYS LOOK
LOVELY — ROALD DAHL

DATE:

HAIR COLOUR:

WHAT HAPPENED:

I DON'T LOVE STUDYING. I HATE STUDYING. I LIKE LEARNING.
LEARNING IS BEAUTIFUL. – NATALIE PORTMAN

DATE:
HAIR COLOUR:
WHAT HAPPENED:

MOST GREAT LEARNING HAPPENS IN GROUPS. COLLABORATION
IS THE STUFF OF GROWTH. — SIR KEN ROBINSON

DATE:

HAIR COLOUR:

WHAT HAPPENED:

FORGIVENESS DOES NOT CHANGE THE PAST, BUT IT DOES
ENLARGE THE FUTURE. — PAUL BOESE

DATE:

HAIR COLOUR:

WHAT HAPPENED:

WHEN YOU TALK, YOU ARE ONLY REPEATING SOMETHING YOU
KNOW. BUT IF YOU LISTEN, YOU MAY LEARN SOMETHING NEW.
— DALAI LAMA

DATE:

HAIR COLOUR:

WHAT HAPPENED:

LEARN AS MUCH AS YOU CAN WHILE YOU ARE YOUNG, SINCE
LIFE BECOMES TOO BUSY LATER - DANA STEWART SCOTT

DATE:

HAIR COLOUR:

WHAT HAPPENED:

THE CAPACITY TO LEARN IS A GIFT; THE ABILITY TO LEARN
IS A SKILL; THE WILLINGNESS TO LEARN IS A CHOICE. -
BRIAN HERBERT

DATE:

HAIR COLOUR:

WHAT HAPPENED:

WORRY IS A MISUSE OF THE IMAGINATION. — DAN ZADRA

DATE:

HAIR COLOUR:

WHAT HAPPENED:

LOGIC WILL TAKE YOU FROM A TO B. IMAGINATION WILL
TAKE YOU EVERYWHERE. - ALBERT EINSTEIN

DATE:

HAIR COLOUR:

WHAT HAPPENED:

BE YOURSELF, FOR EVERYBODY ELSE IS ALREADY TAKEN. -
OSCAR WILDE

DATE:

HAIR COLOUR:

WHAT HAPPENED:

NEVER GIVE UP ON WHAT YOU REALLY WANT TO DO. THE
PERSON WITH BIG DREAMS IS MORE POWERFUL THAN ONE
WITH ALL THE FACTS. — ALBERT EINSTEIN.

DATE:

HAIR COLOUR:

WHAT HAPPENED:

YOU'RE BRAVER THAN YOU BELIEVE AND STRONGER THAN YOU
SEEM, AND SMARTER THAN YOU THINK. — CHRISTOPHER ROBIN

DATE:

HAIR COLOUR:

WHAT HAPPENED:

IN ANY MOMENT OF DECISION, THE BEST THING YOU CAN DO
IS THE RIGHT THING. THE WORST THING YOU CAN DO IS
NOTHING. — THEODORE ROOSEVELT

DATE:

HAIR COLOUR:

WHAT HAPPENED:

DO YOUR LITTLE BIT OF GOOD WHERE YOU ARE; IT'S THOSE
LITTLE BITS OF GOOD PUT TOGETHER THAT OVERWHELM THE
WORLD. — DESMOND TUTU

DATE:

HAIR COLOUR:

WHAT HAPPENED:

THREE THINGS IN HUMAN LIFE ARE IMPORTANT: THE FIRST IS
TO BE KIND; THE SECOND IS TO BE KIND, AND THE THIRD IS
TO BE KIND — HENRY JAMES

DATE:

HAIR COLOUR:

WHAT HAPPENED:

WHEN YOU ARE KIND TO OTHERS, IT NOT ONLY CHANGES YOU,
IT CHANGES THE WORLD — HAROLD KUSHNER

DATE:

HAIR COLOUR:

WHAT HAPPENED:

NOT ONLY MUST WE BE GOOD, BUT WE MUST ALSO BE GOOD
FOR SOMETHING — HENRY DAVID THOREAU

DATE:

HAIR COLOUR:

WHAT HAPPENED:

YESTERDAY IS HISTORY. TOMORROW IS A MYSTERY. TODAY IS A GIFT. THAT'S WHY WE CALL IT 'THE PRESENT' - ELEANOR ROOSEVELT

DATE:

HAIR COLOUR:

WHAT HAPPENED:

A LEADER IS ONE WHO KNOWS THE WAY, GOES THE WAY
AND SHOWS THE WAY — JOHN C. MAXWELL

DATE:

HAIR COLOUR:

WHAT HAPPENED:

IF YOUR ACTIONS INSPIRE OTHERS TO DREAM MORE, LEARN MORE, DO MORE AND BECOME MORE, YOU ARE A LEADER. — JOHN QUINCY ADAMS

DATE:

HAIR COLOUR:

WHAT HAPPENED:

I NEVER THOUGHT IN TERMS OF BEING A LEADER. I THOUGHT
  VERY SIMPLY IN TERMS OF HELPING PEOPLE. — JOHN HUME

DATE:

HAIR COLOUR:

WHAT HAPPENED:

ITS OK, SOMETIMES, TO HAVE A BLUE DAY — CHRIS DUKE

DATE:

HAIR COLOUR:

WHAT HAPPENED:

Lisa and Chris Duke are a husband and wife team behind "Lucy's Blue Day".

Chris has experienced mental health issues throughout his life and into adulthood. He wrote "Lucy's Blue Day" to help children understand "it's ok not to be ok" and it's good to talk.

Lisa has supported Chris through his struggles, after educating herself on mental health and wants to help Chris break the stigma associated with it.

The original "Lucy's Blue Day" started as a poem intended for their eldest daughter. It was only after Lisa read it and suggested it be turned into a children's book and they started crowdfunding to pay for the illustrator that they realised the support from strangers and celebrities alike who wished for a copy too.

Dr Ranj from CBeebies' "Get Well Soon" - "it's a great little book on child mental health."
Stephen Fry - "Charming."
Lorraine Kelly - "It's such a clever, common-sense and totally relatable way to talk about mental health."

Lisa and Chris married in November 2010 and have three daughters together, Alyssa, Summer and Erica.
Chris is working on releasing his first children's novel "Archie Unplugs the Internet" at the end of 2019.

www.lucysblueday.com

Lucy is a very special little girl with magical hair. It changes colour with her emotions. If she is feeling happy, it is purple. If she is jealous, it will turn green. This charming story is the tale of when Lucy wakes up and her hair is blue, and she doesn't understand why. She soon learns that it is #OKNotToBeOK

www.lucysblueday.com

Printed in Poland
by Amazon Fulfillment
Poland Sp. z o.o., Wrocław

55016668R00060